MUSIC WARS

If battles over contemporary worship services cause Christians to split now, will we also have separate services in heaven? How should believers handle the controversy over drums vs. pipe organ?

Presented by
LONNIE MELASHENKO

Written by
DAVID B. SMITH

The Voice of Prophecy

Pacific Press® Publishing Association
Nampa, Idaho
Oshawa, Ontario, Canada

Edited by Jerry D. Thomas
Cover design by Tim Larson
Cover photo © 2000 Erik Stenbakken

Copyright © 2000 by
Pacific Press® Publishing Association
Printed in the United States of America
All Rights Reserved

ISBN 0-8163-1824-7

00 01 02 03 04 • 5 4 3 2 1

Contents

Throwing Rocks at Rock Church 5

If I Dislike It, It Must be Wrong 11

Weird Tunes From Thailand 17

Who Wants to Hear "Les Miz"? 23

Caviar and Crackers 29

Plink, Plink, Plink 35

"Let's Hear It for Ted on the Trumpet!" 41

Zombie Listeners 47

Song Services at Dodger Stadium 53

Two Tents at Camp Meeting 59

Throwing Rocks at Rock Church

There's a very nice church in Birmingham, Alabama that I'm going to pick on a little bit. On the one hand, I'm envious of the fact that Vestavia Hills United Methodist Church has 5,000 members and a thriving program. That beats my Ojai Valley Adventist Church by about 4,950 members, unless you count the Voice of Prophecy radio audience as a congregation. But on any given Sunday, from what is described in the magazine *Christianity Today*, Vestavia Hills has ended up being split into a total of six separate, distinct congregations.

Now, what caused these divisions? Why'd the pie get sliced up six ways? Was there a doctrinal debate and the secret-rapture premillennialists all decided to meet at 8:00 in the morning? Did gay marriage or some other "liberal" issue divide the Body of Christ?

No, actually, it's worked out this way. Every Sunday morning at 8:30 there's a worship service provided in what we would call a traditional style. "The Old Rugged Cross." "Abide With Me." Songs like those, written by legends like Fannie Crosby or Charles Wesley, accompanied by the organ and a small choir. An hour later, the

6 MUSIC WARS

church quickly empties out, and a new group comes in. They're more casually dressed, a bit younger. They use a piano and sometimes a guitar, and do a mild "praise-and-worship" service, flavored with some Southern gospel songs like "I'll Fly Away." And—hold onto your cowboy hat here—they project song lyrics onto the screen with an overhead projector.

Now, Congregation #2 only gets one hour in the sanctuary too, because at 11:00 the ushers push folks out and pull new people in, this time for some more traditional hymns with the organ and a bigger church choir. However, at the same time, 11:00 A.M., in another part of the building, a 300-seat fellowship hall is filling up with young adults and kids; they're getting ready for the "Son Shine" service. Some members at Vestavia Hills call this particular service, either with an approving smile or a tight grimace, the "Rock & Roll Church." And it really is; according to *Christianity Today* writer Michael S. Hamilton, the song list ranges from the new contemporary favorite "I Will Call Upon the Lord" to an old top-40 hit entitled "Jesus Is Just Alright With Me" by none other than the Doobie Brothers.

Well, we're only up to four pie slices so far, and it's not even time for the Sunday potluck. At 5:00 P.M., about 60 retirement-age people gather for Vespers. (Remember that cobweb-covered word?) "I Come to the Garden Alone" and other songs like that, from the good old Methodist *Cokesbury Hymnal*, and just a piano for accompaniment. Then at 7:00 P.M. the amplifiers really get plugged in as Youth Worship cranks into full volume. Nothing but teenagers doing all the latest CCM favorites—that's "Contemporary Christian Music"—along with doctored songs from Billboard's hottest hits, where the lyrics are tweaked to have a bit of Christianity to them. The music is "amplified, raucous, and very loud." According to church member Lee Benson, it's a service "not for the faint of heart."

And there we have it. One church, but SIX completely different, completely distinct congregations holding forth there in praise to God. Is this all right? Is it according to heaven's blueprint? Of course, when you have a 5,000-member church in a sanctuary that only seats 700 at a time, you're going to have to cut up the pie according to some guidelines. But is music the way to do it?

I pose this hard question because all over America, and even around the world, music has become the great dividing line. Dr. Hamilton, professor of history at Notre Dame University, who did this cover article for *Christianity Today* (July 12, 1999), and who writes from his vantage point, concludes: "Vestavia Hills is living evidence that American churchgoers no longer sort themselves out by denomination so much as by musical preference."

In other words, more and more people aren't deciding: "I'll go to this church because it's a Baptist church and I'm a Baptist." Or, "I'll go to this Seventh-day Adventist church"—to use my own faith community—"because in my own Bible studies I find validity in the teachings and the doctrinal perspectives of the Adventist religion." No. People are now saying: "I'll go to that white church on the corner—never mind who's running it—because they have synthesizers, drums, and the song lyrics on a 60-inch TV using Microsoft PowerPoint visuals." Or "I'll go to that other white church on the other corner because they *don't* have all that stuff; they're still singing the good old songs I knew as a kid, songs with names like Isaac Watts at the top."

8   MUSIC WARS

In fact, if you leaf through the Yellow Pages, you'll see at the very top of some of the display ads for churches: "Lively contemporary music." Or: "We sing the traditional favorites." Or, probably most common of all, the Vestavia Hills approach: "Traditional services at these hours, and all the heavy-metal music provided at these other hours." In that same *Christianity Today* article, Dr. Hamilton observes: "Some large churches, like Vestavia Hills, are able to hold the new sects together under one roof. Churches that are too small to sustain separate congregations with separate worship styles are either trying to mix musical styles ('blended worship'), or they are fighting and dividing over which music to use."

And those two words, "fighting" and "dividing" describe what's happening in literally thousands of Christian churches right now; they're fighting and dividing over the issue of music. Churches are splitting right down the middle. Congregations are yelling at their pastors and at each other. Young Christians and old Christians are angry, each with the other. Some believers simply leave; they look in the Yellow Pages and they find a church offering the kind of music they like. Others don't even do that; they go home and play the music they prefer on their own CD players at the house, and they just don't GO to church any longer.

In my own church family, the editor of our church paper, the *Adventist Review*, recently wrote an exceptional editorial on this very topic. Pastor Bill Johnsson is an incredibly gifted writer and theologian, a great, Spirit-filled man with decades of service and experience. And he led into his editorial with this insight: "If there's a topic guaranteed to make young saints angry and old saints apoplectic, it's this one—contemporary Christian music."

That is absolutely *the* truth, isn't it?

When the Voice of Prophecy shared these messages on the radio, we took as our series title: TWO HEAVENS. Vestavia Hills United Methodist Church has split into separate groups over music style. Just about 15 miles from our radio studios, the Thousand Oaks Seventh-day Adventist Church now operates a somewhat traditional service at 11:15 Saturday mornings, while over in a separate building you can hear the insistent beat from "The Place." All the kids go there to hear Place Praise, the worship band. Parents in the main sanctuary; kids at "The Place." Two separate churches.

One of these days, in the sweet by and by, will heaven be held in two seperate places? Will those who want stained glass and a pipe organ enter the building on the right, while those halo-wearing saints who want to play their electric guitars on the sea of glass look for a plug and a PA jack over on the left?

It may be helpful to notice a couple of points from probably the most musical book in the Bible. In Psalms 147:1, King David has this to say, and who could argue? *"How good it is to sing praises to our God, how pleasant and fitting to praise him!"*

I could get a whole sermon right there, but please mark down with me that our music in the sanctuary is meant to give praise to God. Music, whether it's by Fanny Crosby or Jars of Clay, is for the purpose of saying to God: "We love You. We worship You. We adore You. We want to live lives of obedience to You, Jesus." AND it should be pleasant to praise God in that way. Music in church should give us joy and happiness; it should satisfy our souls and give us a spirit of heaven. Notice again: *"How pleasant AND FITTING to praise him!"* David writes.

So it is appropriate and good and necessary that we should go to the churches of our choosing and sing songs there. It's fitting to do that. It should be pleasant to do that. If the music at church is making you mad, then something is seriously wrong.

But hold your finger on that word "pleasant" and go back just 14 verses to another psalm, also by King David. This is Psalms 133, and he opens with this observation: *"How good and pleasant it is when brothers live together IN UNITY!"* (Emphasis supplied.)

What do you think of that? "In unity"? A church may prayerfully decide to split itself up six ways and allow some different praise styles and musical genres in those six new mini-congregations. But that decision, that vote, should be made in a spirit of happy, cheerful unity. It's good and pleasant, David writes, to be in unity.

What to do, then, when the drums on the platform and the Roland synthesizers in the youth chapel lead to DISunity? Stay tuned.

If I Dislike It, It Must be Wrong

There are four words today that are ripping through the world of church. Four words are pitting one Christian against another, dividing parent and child, husband and wife, youth group against senior-citizen group. And the four words are these: "I HATE that music!"

Picture the scene where congregations are splitting into sections. The traditional worship service is over *here*, maybe at 8:30 in the morning. Then at ten, in *this* building, there are drums and keyboards and enough electrical wires and cables and speakers and monitors and flashing lights to accommodate a Madonna concert at Madison Square Garden. The Fanny Crosby fans walk by, see the amps and feel the vibration of the beat as kids sing "All Things Are Possible." And they say to each other: "I hate that music."

Of course, maybe the people who like contemporary music are saying about the slower stuff, "*I* hate THAT music." Meaning that it goes both ways.

Well, right now my own shoulders are sagging just a bit, because one of the sources I generally turn to a lot here on the Voice of Prophecy has just absolutely failed us. I mean, he has let us down completely! Fortunately, I'm not talking about one of the writers in the Bible. But the late, great Christian writer, C. S. Lewis, has been a valuable resource over the years. So often we've turned to great classic books of his like *Mere Christianity*, or *The Four Loves*. And his insights, just about 99.9% of the time, are so solid, so blessed by God with wisdom and biblical integrity.

But now, in a study about the biblical issue of music and worship, I find that Mr. Clive Staples Lewis completely lets us down. Because this brilliant, dedicated, wise Christian scholar simply hated all Christian music! All of it! He hated all of it! If it had drums, he hated it. If it had pipe organs, he hated it. Piano—hate. Stained glass—hate. Orchestra—hate. Long hymns . . . he hated them. Short ones—hated 'em. Praise songs—not invented yet when he was alive, but he would have hated them. For whatever reason, this Cambridge- and Oxford-educated and bred "don," this brilliant little man looked down his nose at all church music and hated all of it. He honestly thought all of it was lousy.

Maybe you're saying: "Oh, come on, you're overstating it." All right. Let me share with you from his own pen what he has to say. In an interview dating back to 1944, which admittedly is before Michael W. Smith and Sixpence None the Richer came along, someone asked him: "Is attendance at a place of worship or membership with a Christian community necessary to a Christian way of life?"

That's a very appropriate question as millions of us mutter out in the parking lot: "I hate that music!" But C. S. Lewis, with all his Ph.Ds makes this admission, word for word: "I disliked very much their hymns [in church], which *I* considered to be fifth-rate poems set to sixth-rate music."

Ouch! Is that a stinger? "Fifth-rate poems set to sixth-rate music." Week after week, he would sit there in the chapels or cathedrals of England and sigh to himself about the songs. He just thought they were junky, inferior music. It set his teeth on edge.

Another time a well-meaning person asked him what he thought could be improved about church. (How we all light up with that kind of a survey!) Again, this great Christian writer, whose words are usually such a beacon to us, kind of sniffed: "What I, like many laymen, chiefly desire in church are fewer, better, and shorter hymns; especially fewer."

Very clearly, here was a man who often said to himself or to others: "Dash it all, I hate that music!"

I'll return a few stanzas later in the hymnal to our pompous, nose-in-the-air friend Mr. Lewis and see if he himself decided to quit going to church because the music was so bad. There are some very valuable lessons we can learn from a confession he makes later in the same interview. But I invite you to consider three responses to the issue of: "I hate that music." More specifically, this very human reaction: "That music is wrong because I hate it." Or "evil." Or "should be banned." All around the world, good, sincere Christians are convinced that music being played in their church is displeasing to God and that the amps ought to be unplugged.

Here are the three points, and the first one is a concession. I can only speak for me as I read my Bible and spin my CDs and go to my church. But yes, I'm convinced that there is music being played today that is antithetical to, or against, the principles of true Christian worship. Is there rock-and-roll music that is wrong, that is tainted by sinfulness? I believe there is. Is there music that displeases God? I believe there is. Is that music sometimes played in church? Sometimes, yes.

Back to that brilliant, warm, encompassing article in the *Adventist Review*. Bill Johnsson, after reaching out to these various groups, concedes: "I have no doubt that some music in Adventist churches has gone beyond the bounds."

He goes on to point out that some of the "praise music" being sung today in our churches is, as it seems to him, "shallow . . . in both tunes and words."

A much stronger opinion is being registered by another book floating around in my denomination just now. According to Samuele Bacchiocchi: "Rock and roll is not just a musical style, but a revolutionary religious movement." A bit later: "Rock music is not just another musical genre that can be sanitized to worship God and proclaim the Gospel. A closer look at the rock scene reveals that rock and roll embodies an endtime apostate religious movement of open rebellion against God and the moral principles revealed in His word."

And later in the same volume comes this criticism: "The mixture of good and evil in rock music may well represent an effective satanic strategy to use the good lyrics to lead some Christians to accept more readily the evil ones."

Of course, no one book can solve the issue of what music ought to, or ought not to, be played and sung in our churches. And not on a radio program or in ten years of radio programs. The issue here is: What do we do when we hate church music, and, Is it possible that some music ought to be hated? From where I'm sitting today, the answer to that first question must prayerfully be a Yes. There is music that does not belong in a Christian setting, a worship experience where we want Christ to be uplifted, God to be exalted, and the Holy Spirit to be present.

But question number two is this: Is it possible to believe that music is wrong, or sinful, or inappropriate—perhaps not because we know enough to know that for sure—but simply because we don't like that music? Is that possible? Is it possible to quickly go from "I hate that music" to "Everyone should hate that music. That is bad music."

In the same very well-written *Christianity Today* article entitled "Triumph of the Praise Songs: How Guitars Beat Out the Organ in the Worship Wars," Michael S. Hamilton makes this point: "Every complaint about worship music, no matter which style, claims to be rooted in theological principles. Yet in every critique, the theology aligns perfectly with the critic's own musical taste."

What's he saying here? A critic says: "The rap music genre is inherently evil. It has no place in church." Question: "Do you personally LIKE rap music?" Answer: "Heavens, no. I hate it." Ah. Is that a coincidence? The point is that not liking something and condemning it might often go hand in hand.

However, I might argue with the writer of this article just a bit. I have no doubt that there are musicians who, to pick an example, have succeeded in the rock-and-roll culture. For years they've liked it, performed it, lived, and breathed it. And then, as God moves upon their heart, they feel led to reject at least some forms of the very music that all their lives they have enjoyed and had an affinity for. In their inward souls, they like it still . . . and yet they see the fruits, the results, of some kinds of rock music, and spiritually ask God to help them put it out of their lives. That would be a tough battle, and yet one we all should consider in our own lives.

Still, as the noise of battle surrounds us in our church parking lots, and in our youth fellowship halls, it might be well for us to join C. S. Lewis in realizing: "Just because *I* don't like this music isn't an ironclad guarantee that it's wrong everywhere, every day, for everyone."

Bill Johnsson, in his editorial, writes about this new music: "This is sound from somewhere else, which I do not understand and but faintly appreciate." But then he adds: "What I appreciate is the fervent love for Jesus that I see in the young people who do understand and appreciate it. I covet their spirit of commitment to Christ and His mission. Seeing them, knowing them, I cannot write off their music, dismiss it with simplistic taglines."

Weird Tunes From Thailand

Have you ever taken along your little portable AM/FM radio on a trip to a very foreign country? Maybe in your overseas hotel room, eight time zones away, you managed to figure out the voltage converter and you plugged in your own radio from back home and tried to scan the dial to see what was on there in that distant place?

Here in the 21st century, the way the world is shrinking, and the way people everywhere can pull the latest hits right off the Internet, you might hear the exact same songs they're playing on KIIS FM back home in L.A. On the other hand, I've done enough traveling around this globe of ours to know that there's a lot of music in other countries that sounds just plain other-worldly to this California native. Music from South America has its own unique rhythm. Songs they play in the hill tribes of Northern Thailand, I discovered during a recent mission trip to the land of my childhood, are played on rather interesting instruments with rather interesting scales. Around the world, there are radio hits, and cassettes, and CDs, and MP3 recordings of music that, unless you live in that culture . . . well, you can hardly make heads or tails out of it. In a word, it is strange.

On the one hand, you might like it because it's strange. You're adventuresome; you try new music the way you try new restaurants. But I suppose there are many of the rest of us who get back to Los Angeles International Airport, get back to our car, flip on the radio, lean back in the seat and say: "Aaaaah. Now THAT'S music!"

Christian churches everywhere are being sliced right down the middle by the "praise-and-worship" music wars. Contemporary music is invading the territory of the saints; amplifiers and drums and overhead transparencies are replacing pipe organs, choir robes, and hymnals. And while some of those who are resisting the tidal wave of change are simply sighing: "I hate that music!", there are others who are using the "S" word for it. And the "S" doesn't stand for "synthesizer" or "Steven Curtis Chapman." To them, S is for SIN, and S is for SATANIC, and S is for "Someone please get those drums out of MY church."

Let me confess that I do not make light of that feeling. At the Voice of Prophecy, we've wrestled on our knees for 70 years over what music is acceptable to play in this cathedral we call Christian radio. Our music committee has put some songs on the shelf because we didn't think they would please the Lord. In our Family Reunion Concerts, which are pure joy to participate in, there have been endless hours of discussion about this song or that one. Would God be honored or not honored by the contemporary track on such-and-such musician's chosen solo? The question of "sin" when it comes to Christian music is one every believer needs to honestly face up to in his or her own walk with the God who created the gift of music.

Again, let's face the reality that there is music which belongs in worship, and music that doesn't. Music is not a neutral thing; not all forms of music can be baptized and brought into the sanctuary. And we do need to explore some principles we can consider in making those hard, hard decisions.

However, here is a "counterbalancing" point: it doesn't always hold true that anything you or I might find to be "strange" is necessarily out of place in Christian worship.

In John Stott's book, *The Contemporary Christian*, he writes with a bit of bemusement about how his own Anglican Church tried to take the gospel message to some of the countries of Africa. He was baffled to find the native clerics perspiring in agony, dressed "to the nines" in the full robes and regalia the priests back in England were wearing. Out in the desolate reaches of Africa were these tall, stone spires, these cathedrals that looked as if they belonged on the Thames River. Stone cathedrals. Scarlet robes. Pipe organs. And all around them, in the 95 degree heat, was Africa. The simple, pure joy, the elementary faith of good African men and women, being smothered by the "correct" forms of worship imported from Stratford-upon-Avon.

Would the tunes and instrumentations of Africa have sounded strange to Stott? Probably so. On the other hand, did the funereal sounds of the pipe organs probably sound strange to the farmers and the goat herders from the little villages? Of course they did. And what both sides had to realize, and what we all have to realize today, is that if something seems "strange" to us, that doesn't for sure mean that it is universally wrong for everyone.

In that *Adventist Review* editorial by Bill Johnsson, he has this to say about his study of the so-called worship wars: "I learned much: that sincere Christians . . . respond to music in sharply divergent manners. That music that sounds strange to my ears may become a vehicle for devotion, adoration, and praise to Jesus as Saviour and Lord."

Let me ask myself a question right here. Am I completely sure that I can tell when something "strange" is also inappropriate and wrong? Have my views over what is "strange" ever changed in the past 45 years of life? As a Christian, are there things that seem perfectly normal and wonderful to me, which, to an outsider looking in, might seem strange?

In a very well-written book a few years ago entitled *Surprised By the Power of the Spirit*, author Jack Deere discusses very frankly some of the controversial facets of today's charismatic movement. Speaking in tongues. Miracles. Healings. And sometimes a person will reject unusual manifestations happening in a church because they seem so strange. Downright weird. Pastor Deere is the first one to confess that abuses do happen; things take place that God doesn't direct or control. We need to be careful and prayerful. But then he adds this observation, which has huge relevance as all of us carefully and prayerfully try to decide what kinds of music we should admit to the house of God.

"Strangeness is not a criterion for truth," he writes. "Nor is it a criterion we would want to use in order to decide whether something is scriptural or unscriptural." Then he adds: "There is much in Scripture that is exceedingly strange. The prophet Isaiah, for example, went naked and barefoot for three years as a sign against

Egypt and Cush (Isaiah 20:3). The prophet Hosea was commanded to marry a prostitute (Hosea 1:2). The dead bones of Elisha actually raised the dead (2 Kings 13:21). Peter's shadow healed the sick person on which it fell (Acts 5:15). Handkerchiefs and aprons that touched Paul's body healed the sick and drove out demons (Acts 19:12)."

Pastor Deere continues to take us into the mysterious book of Revelation. "Suppose I were to tell you that I had a vision in which I saw the throne of God. In my vision there were four living creatures resembling a lion, a calf, a man, and an eagle, each of whom had six wings and were filled with eyes all around and within them. These creatures were saying, 'Holy, holy, holy' as they flew around the throne of God day and night. Who would believe that this was a legitimate vision if it had not already been written in Revelation 4:6-8?"

He summarizes: "I am not saying that we ought to believe every strange thing that is told to us." You and I could add: "Or accept as sacred every strange tune that someone brings into the front door of the church." But, Pastor Deere concludes: "I AM saying, however, that nothing should be discounted as untrue or unscriptural simply because it is strange."

Consider this very familiar scenario. A totally secular person, an atheist, let's say, who has lived his whole life apart from the symbols and the trappings of church, peeks in through a window. Inside, he sees people dunking one another in a little pool of water. "What in the world is that?" he wonders. A moment later, he sees whole rows of people, all holding the tiniest little cups of what look like root beer. Or something. And they have little crackers, it looks like. They are muttering something over these tiny, insignificant, inadequate snacks. Then they eat them, their eyes closed, their lips moving. Now, if you're a born-again Christian like me, the Lord's Supper, or Communion, is a wonderful blessing. It's not strange! It's the symbol of the body and blood of Jesus shed for us, for our sins. It has meaning. It has value. But to that Wall Street tycoon, that scientifically-trained atheist looking through the window, it is weirdness of the highest magnitude.

It's no wonder that Jack Deere closes out his essay with this quiet observation from the great John Wesley: "From this time, I trust, we shall all suffer God to carry on His own work in the way that pleaseth Him."

Who Wants to Hear "Les Miz"?

It's one of the finest musical expressions there is, composed by the French genius Alain Boublil. *Les Misérables*—often dubbed "The world's favorite musical," based on the book by Victor Hugo, of course. And some of the best songs in the three-hour Broadway performance are done by the character Jean Valjean. This past December in Los Angeles, down at the Ahmanson Theater, a brilliant tenor named Ivan Rutherford performed all his solos, bringing down the house with "Who Am I?", "Bring Him Home," and leading the chorus in "One Day More." This is high-brow, classically excellent material approved by the world's greatest musical critics.

On the other hand, I suppose that right down the street from the Ahmanson there must be a bar or two where men in working-class clothes gather after a hard ten hours of work. And after a few drinks, they probably start to sway around there in the bar, and they begin to bellow out the old favorites like "Can't Take My Eyes Off of You" or "My Girl." Off-key, off-beat . . . and off limits to some of us who are trying to keep our bloodstreams alcohol-free and our minds junk-free.

But here we have the high and the low. A man in a tuxedo, or wearing the mayor's clothes in the role of Jean Valjean, singing in operatic perfection. And in the pub, working-class stiffs are belching out their own boozy favorites. Is it music on both ends? Is it acceptable on both ends?

I have to return, with a bit of impatience, perhaps, to the views of Christian writer C. S. Lewis regarding church music. To him, sitting in the founder's circle of London's finest opera houses, all church music was lowbrow. He hated all of it. I already shared his disdainful quote about church music, but here it is again in all its sarcastic, slicing splendor: "Fifth-rate poems set to sixth-rate music."

Lewis would sit in church on a Sunday morning and look around him at all the common people. Not too well-dressed, some of them. Uneducated, perhaps. And undoubtedly, a few of them would go right from the church to the nearest pub, play a round of darts, have a pint or two, and begin to sing "My Gal Sal" in the same tone as they had just done the hymns at church. In fact, C. S. Lewis described the average congregational song on a Sunday morning as "people shouting their favorite hymns." "The lusty roar of the congregation." And he was not impressed.

He points out, though, as he examines his own soul, that all of us tend to look from our musical camp over to the other side . . . and sniff. Oh brother! How in the world can they listen to *that?* Jean Valjean looks down at the beer-swilling riffraff with their campfire songs and just shakes his head. He wouldn't wish their music on his worst enemy, Javert. The Bowery Boys, on the other hand, look at the poster where Monsieur Valjean's got on his fancy-schmancy tuxedo and his opera hair, and they shake their heads too. How in tarnation can anybody spend sixty bucks to hear that lacy-legato stuff? Go figure.

Of course, this division exists within our churches too. Some congregations embrace what we call a "high-church" creed: classical music, a pipe organ. A paid minister of music with a Ph.D. The choirs have their music carefully chosen by someone who can trace the background of the hymn, making sure they don't unwittingly use something that came out of a European beer garden.

At the Voice of Prophecy, we've actually had letters and phone calls coming from some of the finest universities in my own denomination. People in the music department, urging us here in our radio ministry to stay strictly within the confines of the very pure. "Don't let down your guard," they say.

On the other hand . . . we have the other hand. The left hand wants something with a common touch. A bit of Southern Gospel. A bit of guitar. A bit of beat. "I'll Fly Away." "Turn Your Radio On." And, speaking of the "shouting of the congregation," I can't help but notice that one of the most popular "praise-and-worship" songs being sung right now in tens of thousands of Christian churches is entitled "Shout to the Lord." It's actually a very good song, but not done with a pipe organ as accompaniment. And my point is this: there are these groups out there—both probably convinced that they're right. Both convinced that their side ought to win. Both sides probably disdaining the other side.

Back for a moment to our high-falutin' friend, Clive Staples Lewis, who sneered at the common folks with their common, plaid-coat church songs. "Christ is coming in the sky. I will see Him by and by." That kind of thing, and he thought it was pure junk. However, he finally makes a confession about his own feelings: "I disliked very much their hymns. . . . But as I went on I saw the great merit of it. I came up against different people of quite different outlooks and different education, and then gradually my conceit just began peeling off. I realized that the hymns (which were just sixth-rate music) were, nevertheless, being sung with devotion and benefit by an old saint in elastic-side boots in the opposite pew, and then you realize that you aren't fit to clean those boots." And then this poignant confession: "It [the music, the humility] gets you out of your solitary conceit."

Maybe all of us need a dose of that humility as we try to resolve these music wars. If all your life you've been to high church, or to a place of worship where the traditional music has dominated, you're probably very impatient with what's happening now. The guitars, the amplifiers, the lame lyrics. (They seem lame to you, at least. "Shine, Jesus, shine. Shine, Jesus, shine. Shine, Jesus, shine.") But consider the people—maybe young people, maybe teenagers, maybe "seekers" who have never been to church—who are for the first time bringing their talents to the Lord. A young person works for hours with a computer, trying to get the lyrics to the songs up there on a big screen. He spends hours on it. A teenager, just a high school sophomore, has a ponytail and a bass guitar, and the music director says: "Sure! Bring it to practice Thursday night. We'll fit you in. You can play with us."

"Are you sure?" the kid says. "You really want me?" And he rehearses his part. He looks forward to the weekend when he has a part in worship. Can we be humble enough, you and I, to see the devotion in their hearts, the first tiny steps these people are taking toward the kingdom? Can we be humble enough to walk past the youth tent at camp meeting, where we hear the keyboard and the drums, and be glad that people are worshiping there?

And let's go at it from the other side of the coin. Look at that faithful saint who has been in her chosen pew for 60 years. For six decades, she's sung out of the official hymnal. That faded black book in the pew, where "Praise to the Lord" is #1, "On Jordan's Stormy Banks" is #620, and nobody's ever tampered with those numbers, with The Way Things Are. To her, that is music. That is worship. It has meaning to her. And for six decades she has been a vital part of that church—attending, witnessing, inviting, contributing. She could no more relate to a concert by DC Talk than fly to the moon. And yet her Christian experience is valid too.

Can we glance out of our own pew, as C. S. Lewis did, and see the person on the other side? And say to ourselves: "Wait a minute. Maybe I haven't discovered the only formula. Maybe that person's experience is real too. Maybe God can work through a variety of expressions, and within the Body of Christ we need to make room for each other. Maybe, just maybe." Perhaps the fact that there are these "worship wars" is actually a good thing . . . if it serves, as Lewis admitted, to "get us out of our solitary conceit."

Thinking back to our past attitudes, I suppose most of us find that it's two very short steps from: "I like this music," to "*Everyone* should only like this music," to "*God* delights only in this music." And whether you're wearing a $900 evening gown and playing the harp at the Shubert Theater, or banging a tambourine at "The Place," one of our livelier worship services here in the Conejo Valley every Sabbath morning, it's tempting to decide that God's on your side and only your side.

Well, one verse of Scripture at least helps us to look across the aisle. In Psalm 149:3, 4, it's interesting that we find both of those specific instruments mentioned: *"Let them praise his name with dancing and make music to him with tambourine and harp."* Notice: tambourine and harp. And why? *"For the Lord takes delight in his people; he crowns the humble with salvation."*

Poor, resentful, struggling, choking-on-pride C. S. Lewis finally got himself a dose of humility sitting there in church. The little old lady across the way with her cheap elastic-side boots was singin' to Jesus. He finally got humble enough to value that, to honor it. And it's a good thing, says the Bible, because it's the humble that get a crown.

Caviar and Crackers

There was a cute cartoon in *Leadership* magazine not too long ago, and it didn't have a single word of dialogue in the caption. Two preachers are staring silently up at the grand fresco, this great wall of marble. And carved in it are the following words: "Introit. Ministers kneel. Welcome. Hymn of Worship. Offering. Pastoral Prayer. Sermon. Closing Hymn. Benediction."

And that was it. Not a word of discussion, no jokes, or puns, or ha-ha one-liners. Just this order of worship . . . CARVED IN GRANITE. And of course, that was the point. This "way of doing things," or what we call the "liturgy," was carved in stone. The offering comes before the pastoral prayer, it always has come before the pastoral prayer, it always will come before the pastoral prayer . . . and woe betide the person who even clears his throat to suggest a change from that sacred WAY. It will not happen. In my own Adventist denomination, we sometimes joke that such-and-such policy has been dictated down to us "according to the laws of the Medes and Persians, which 'changeth not.' "

And you know, "changeth not" are two words which

sound pretty wonderful to some of the participants in these "music wars." Perhaps you've felt, or wished, that it was carved in stone at your church: "Music will be done with the organ, and only the organ." And we come up, on both sides, against a certain fierce inflexibility.

Poor, unhappy C. S. Lewis really did hate all the music they did at church. Oh, he didn't think it was sinful; the Christian rock group Stryper hadn't come on the scene yet. But week after week, he sat in his pew, looking at the common folks bellowing out their favorite songs—all of them so banal and simplistic, he thought. And it took a while before a certain humility crept over him. He finally began to appreciate the fact that other people were being blessed by this common music; they were finding Jesus Christ through the cheerful singing they were doing each Sunday. Maybe the great cathedrals of London weren't as desecrated as he had thought.

So humility is important for all of us as we look up at the great stone carving, which thunders down: "Music shall always be done in such-and-such a way—thus saith the Lord!" We need to realize that our thoughts and opinions aren't the final answer to every question.

But in other writings of his, C. S. Lewis makes two additional points that are helpful as we continue to grapple with the very real dilemma of music in the church. What do we do when we are unhappy with the choices being made? Where do we turn if we're not being blessed by the guitars and keyboards people are bringing in?

First of all, as Lewis points out, it's a good and common rule at sea if two ships are about to collide: the more maneuverable of the two ought to give way. To back down or turn at least a bit to the side so as to avoid a crash.

What does this mean for us in a new millennium, as pipe organs are giving way to drum sets, and where hymnals are meekly surrendering to the overhead projector and the PowerPoint song lyrics? Many churches are attempting to hold their congregations together with what they call "blended worship." A hymn, then a praise song. A traditional favorite followed by something with a bit of Southern Gospel. And what the pastor and the minister of music are hoping the Christians in the pew will learn to do is to hang in there. Be flexible. If you don't like the song they're singing right this minute, just sit tight. In three minutes, they'll be doing one you do like. "And," the pastor might be saying, "liking music is not the main point anyway. We're here to honor God, not just to like things." Which is a point we need to consider further.

But now the second concept. How true that there are among us "high" musicians and, well, "low" ones. Worshipers who like the pipe organ, and the great composers. And those who like the Maranatha Praise Band and songs like "Everything's Gonna Be All Right in Christ." And both of these groups often tend to look down at the other group. "There but for the grace of God go I." Except that there's not much grace in the confession.

Well, here's the second point from C. S. Lewis, and this comes from a 1948 essay he wrote entitled, ironically, "Correspondence With an Anglican Who Dislikes Hymns."

"There are two musical situations," he writes, "on which I think we can be confident that a blessing rests. One is where a priest or an organist, himself a man of trained and delicate taste, humbly and charitably sacrifices his own (aesthetically right) desires and gives the people humbler and coarser fare than he would wish, in a belief (even, as it may be, the erroneous belief) that he can thus bring them to God."

And there's probably a lot of that happening. A music director with a doctorate and years of university training gives the church family crackers instead of caviar, even though he much prefers caviar. He's got caviar. He likes caviar. He knows, or believes, that caviar is better. But, in order to be a blessing to the cracker-eating public, he quietly lowers himself and gives them crackers. In this case, "common" music.

Here's the rest of Lewis's essay, though. "The other [situation God blesses]," he writes, "is where the stupid and unmusical layman humbly and patiently, and above all silently, listens to music which he cannot, or cannot fully, appreciate, in the belief that it somehow glorifies God, and that if it does not edify him this must be his own defect."

Have you ever been in that camp? You sit in the pew, and the music someone is doing is just miles too high for you. Maybe not even in English. Now, you can tell that it's a well-performed Latin madrigal; it's "high church." But you're not getting heads or tails out of it. And yet, I hope, you quietly sit there, saying to yourself: "This isn't doing it for me. But it does honor God . . . I guess. (He speaks Latin.) And others around me must be getting a taste of heaven out of it, even if the wiring in me doesn't seem to tune this in very well."

Now to the conclusion of C. S. Lewis's essay, and remember that this was hugely personal for him. This is how he reacted too—stuck in a pew at church, listening to music which went right past him, either on the high or the low side. For sure, it wasn't hitting him. But he hung in there and then writes about these two groups who are perhaps frustrated, but who patiently endure for the sake of others. "Neither such a High Brow nor such a Low Brow can be far out of the way. To both, Church Music will have been a means of grace; not the music they have liked, but the music they have disliked. They have both offered, sacrificed, their taste in the fullest sense."

That's a huge challenge, isn't it? To make our musical dissatisfaction a "means of grace." Hanging in there while music you don't care for blesses others. May God help us.

But there's a flip side we have to contend with for sure. What if we block out the grace? The Ph.D. music director looks down in disgust at the masses with their guitars. The kids with the ponytails and the Alesis synthesizers and sound boards look up at the pipe organ with equal disdain. Here's Lewis's final thought about it all: "But where the opposite situation arises, where the musician is filled with the pride of skill or the virus of emulation and looks with contempt on the unappreciative congregation, or where the unmusical, complacently entrenched in their own ignorance and conservatism, look with the restless and resentful hostility of an inferiority complex on all who would try to improve their taste—there, we may be sure, all that both offer is unblessed and the spirit that moves them is not the Holy Ghost."

Here's another inspired bit of that wonderful editorial by Bill Johnsson. After making a number of key points, he concludes with this: "Our big need all around is to respect and appreciate each other, regardless of age, culture, or musical idiom."

In Matthew chapter 26, right after Jesus has the final Passover supper with His disciples, the night before He dies, the Bible tells us they sang a hymn and then left for the Mount of Olives and Gethsemane. And Jesus Christ, who in His prior glory with the Father, had heard the choral praises of millions of adoring angels, cherubic choirs we could never comprehend, who had Himself created all the intricacies of melody and harmony the universe has ever known or ever will know, quietly sang a hymn, blending His voice with the rough, untrained voices of eleven fishers of men. In all the forms of grace He would pour out that weekend, we also have . . . a country song.

Plink, Plink, Plink

My uncle, Morris Venden, tells a marvelous story about a little girl—maybe three years old—who came bursting into her father's office. "Daddy! Daddy! Daddy! I've learned how to write!"

Now, Daddy knew full well that she couldn't write worth a lick; she hadn't even graduated from the sandbox to *Sesame Street* yet. But there in her hand she had a piece of paper covered with all kinds of scribbles and blotches. And she held it up to him. "See?"

Well, he did what most dads do. He began to gush over it. "Wow! Sure enough. You did learn how to write. You go, girl." Or whatever dads said in that neighborhood. "Good job, honey. That's really great writing."

She soaked in his praise for a minute, still grinning from ear to ear. And all of a sudden she sliced right through his false front with this: "What's it say, Daddy? What's it say?"

And the poor guy turned hot and cold all over. "What's it SAY?" Well, it didn't say *anything* . . . but he couldn't tell her that. And she was looking up at her wonderful daddy, this icon of truthfulness and hope. "What's it say,

Daddy?" And as Venden tells the story, God must have given this dad wisdom from heaven, because he scooped his daughter up in his lap and told her. "Well, sweetie, it says here that you're a little girl. And you're trying to learn how to write. And you're just getting started, but one of these days you're going to be able to write really well. Poems and stories and books and everything." And he gave her a big squeeze. "That's what it says."

And the kid can't believe it. "It does?"

"Yes."

It's a sweet story, isn't it? And Venden helps us to see ourselves in the picture, where we do some little good deeds, some little smidgen of obedience, and we're so happy and we go rushing to God. "Hey, God! Lookit! I've learned how to obey!" And God sees these tiny little efforts of ours, these oh-so-human endeavors, where our so-called goodness just barely measures a *blip* on His screen, where we cast the smallest shadow beneath the glory of His eternal Ten Commandments. But in kindness, He looks down and says to us, "Yes! You are trying to obey! Your heart is right. You're doing your best. And one of these days, if you stay in friendship with Me, I'm going to help you to know and experience the real thing."

Well, how does this connect up with "music wars," where people who like "Onward Christian Soldiers" and people who like Audio Adrenaline look across the great divide at each other, and some of them actually pick up swords and spears? Spiritual ones, at least.

The fundamental question that every single believer has to answer, of course, is this one: it's not hugely important what we think of our music; after all, we human beings have notoriously twisted taste, don't we? We've proved that with our *TV Guides*, our diets, our vocabularies, and the whole nine yards. If we like our music a certain way in church, that wouldn't really prove anything at all. But the question is this: What does GOD think of our music? Whether it's by Fanny Crosby, or Philips, Craig, and Dean?

I'd like to put off just a bit longer any discussion about the morality of my favorite music, or of your favorite music. But is it even good? Is it grand and glorious to God? Impressive? Well performed?

Certainly all of us have run into the buzz saw of badly done music at church. Kids get up there with their plug-in guitars and their microphones—with all the cables and the feedback and the one singer that's way louder than the rest. And the drummer who can't keep time. And an old man like me sits in the back row, 45 years old and getting older by the second as that bass guitar's thumps go right through my spleen. And the music is just plain bad. I know it's bad. Everyone knows it's bad. Surely God must know it's bad.

And on the other side, I'm sure there are little country Baptist churches, and Methodist churches—and I can testify that I've been in enough Adventist churches—where even the traditional music was just not very well done. The organ was reedy, out-of-tune, too loud, too soft, too broken . . . which meant we sang a cappella that Sabbath. The choir leader didn't show up. The PA didn't work. Everyone in the alto section was consistently off-key. It reminds us of that church bulletin where the sermon title was announced: "What and Where Is Hell?" And right below, it said: "Come early and listen to our choir practice!"

Well, let me stop being so negative. Let's go to some of the finest church choirs in the country. Let's go to Willow Creek Community Church. Let's go to Saddleback. First Baptist in Dallas. Let's go to Loma Linda University Seventh-day Adventist Church, or to Westminster Abbey. Put on the stage one of the top-notch Christian praise bands, or the finest classical organist, or the unforgettable choir from Azusa Pacific University. Now, that's good stuff. God would surely be impressed by THAT. Wouldn't He?

But we're forgetting what God has up in heaven, aren't we? We're forgetting the angel choirs—made up of millions of angels—and how they've had thousands of years to compose and rehearse. There's never a false note in heaven. Angels never miss rehearsal. Angels never come to practice with a grudge to nurse, a bit of temper or pique, which sours the face and flattens the notes. That never happens.

And of course, we can't imagine the instruments there. Sounds and chords and progressions and musical motifs that have never been considered on this off-tune little planet; we're just not up to it. Listen, they hear symphonies by the sea of glass that have never entered into the hearts of man; the Bible says so in 1 Corinthians 2. They sing a new song; the book of Revelation says that. Up there, it's music, music, music, 24 hours a day . . . the likes of which words cannot describe and our greatest composers cannot duplicate.

And then, on a very regular basis, God leans over the railing and listens to the feeble *plink plink plink* we offer Him from down here. Guitars and drums. Pipe organs and choirs. High and low. Rock and nonrock. But to the trained ears of heaven, it's pretty much *plink plink plink*.

And yet—I believe this with all my heart—God is

pleased by the music we offer up in worship to Him. Not because it's so good; obviously, He has better channels He can tune into up there. But because it's being offered from hearts that worship and adore and love.

As C. S. Lewis, who admittedly hated all Christian music, makes his own confession, and as he analyzes the worth of our songs, our anthems, or hymns, our choruses, he makes this observation: "All our offerings, whether of music or martyrdom, are like the intrinsically worthless present of a child, which a father values indeed, but values only for the intention."

If you're a dad, you know all about this. Your two-year-old brings you a present for your birthday. And it is just *nothing*. Some ceramic blob, or a picture he colored, or a jar with centipedes from the backyard. Or a grungy little toy he got for you from Pic'n'Save, using your money. "Here, Daddy." And like the father in our opening story, you "oooh" and you "ahhh" and you hug and you praise. Not because the present is wonderful, but because the heart is wonderful. You find beauty in the gift, because the spirit of the giver is right.

There's a story about scribbles and off-key music found in the book of Genesis, chapter four. Actually, this Cain-and-Abel anecdote has to do with offerings brought to God. Abel, the younger son, brought God a lamb from his flock, while Cain, with whatever motivation in mind, brought God some of the fruits out of his garden. Now, did God need the fruit, or the lamb? No. He wasn't hungry, and He already had all the lambs and cattle on a thousand hills. God never needs the things we offer up to Him, whether they're offerings, lambs, or organ preludes. His own storehouses are already full. What's important is the heart we bring along with the gift. And the NIV text notes here in Genesis 4 that for some reason Cain had come to worship with a bad motivation and a bad attitude. Some scholars conjecture that God had already explained to earth's first family the importance of the lamb—pointing forward to the true Lamb of God coming later for their redemption. Over in Hebrews 11, we discover that Abel's offering was better because it was given "by faith."

In any case, the lesson for us is clear. In our gifts of worship to God, of music, our songs and our violins and our guitars—all trinkets and scribblings by heaven's standards—it's the heart that counts. Is humility there? And worship? And faith? Are you bringing your loving Father your very best gift?

If so, He's going to smile and enjoy it. *Plink, plink, plink.*

"Let's Hear It for Ted on the Trumpet!"

It's hot, dark, and sweaty at Preservation Hall or over at the New Orleans Heritage Hall. You've just had a good-and-hot Jambalaya meal at the Cajun Corner, and you've worked off some of that Creole cooking by walking down Rampart Street and from one end of Bourbon to the other. And now you're listening as the musicians tune up their instruments for a night of improvisation and jazz. Maybe a big-name performer like Nelson Rangell is there. Or just a ragtag collection of local musicians: a couple of trumpets, slide trombone, clarinet, big upright bass, piano, a drummer. And they start in with a nine-minute version of "When the Saints Go Marching In" and take it from there.

I've got to confess that I haven't experienced very much of what I just described. Most of the jazz I've heard in my life, I heard at Disneyland from the musicians who wander around from their home base at the New Orleans Square. But I know that some of the best toe-tappin' songs they do over at the Snug Harbor Jazz Club and similar venues in New Orleans can run a good ten or fifteen minutes long. These guys make it look so easy improvising, but it takes years of practice to get that kind of Dixieland music to come out right.

One feature of this kind of music, if you've ever attended a performance, is how on these marathon songs, the spotlight passes from one player to another. After a brief jam session where they're all playing at once, the solo mike goes to the trumpet player. And for 16 or 32 measures, he'll really burn up the valves, while the other players in the band kind of just play background for him. Then the clarinet or the sax takes a crack at it. The "bones" get a turn, followed by the piano player and the drummer. Then, after the audience has whistled and clapped for each of these solo moments, the whole band comes back together for the big finale. But that kind of "pass the pedestal" experience is very common down in New Orleans, or wherever this kind of music is played.

Now there's nothing wrong with performing. You and I attend performances all the time, where a gifted musician puts on a performance. He or she plays; we listen. The spotlight's on them, not us. When it's over, we clap for them, and they stand there bowing. The world of entertainment works that way, and there's nothing inherently evil about it.

What about in church, though? Because that's really the stage for this discussion. When musicians play in church, when they participate in a Christian worship service, is it a performance there? Is there a place for a worship leader to point to the trombone player and cry out to the congregation: "Sammy 'The Slide' Simpson, everyone! Give 'im a hand! All right, Sammy!" Or even: "Peter 'The Pipe Organ' Paulsen! Good job, Pete! Come on, folks! Let's hear it!" How much of that should go on in our churches on Sabbath or Sunday morning?

"LET'S HEAR IT FOR TED ON THE TRUMPET!" 43

There was a great article in the magazine *Ministries Today* a couple of years back. It was written to give guidelines to worship leaders as they direct congregations in today's contemporary song services. So it referred to the keyboards, the guitars, the drums, the mikes, the overhead transparencies, and all the rest. And then it shared with these would-be leaders how to select songs, how to create a flow that would prepare a congregation for the sermon, prepare them for the invitation to accept Christ, get them ready to be touched by the Holy Spirit. There really is a science to the study of Christian music, you know, and this well-written article was clear in explaining how a carefully chosen song menu can be a powerful tool in preparing people's hearts for salvation.

But toward the close of the article this warning was found. The chief objective for that worship leader, the author suggested, was that the congregation should completely forget that he or she is up there on the platform. There would be no "All right, Bill! Great worship set!" None of that. Whether the congregation sang two songs or nine, whether it was upbeat or quiet, contemporary or reflective, the goal would be that all traces of a worship leader's personality would recede into the background. The Holy Spirit would be front and center; the singer and his backup vocalists, the bass player, the keyboard artist, the drummer, the trumpet players—all would fade into the wallpaper, so to speak.

What do you think of that? And of course, we would want this same concept to apply in our traditional services, in our "high church" moments. A great choir director and his 150-voice choir, our finest cathedral organists, our high-quality brass ensembles . . . fading into the background. Our soloists . . . fading into the background. Everything about US . . . fading away.

In reading up on this very fascinating topic, I borrowed from a rather emphatic set of Internet essays that were circulating around in my own denomination just then. And I must confess that there were some very valid points being made in this critique of the presence of rock-and-roll in our Christian churches today. Because this desire for applause, for self-worship, for getting up on pedestals, is one of the things that the author rightly condemns.

Here's just a line from Samuele Bacchiocchi's manuscript—and really, could we argue? "Michael Jackson," he writes, "has carefully staged himself throughout the world as an icon of deity. His videos regularly display him giving erotic gestures to the camera; his extravagantly-rendered stage productions present strong implications of his godhood (manifested in his entrances and exits), lauding him as the savior of the world."

Have you noticed any of that? Maybe you remember a Super Bowl halftime show a few years ago where Jackson was the featured presenter. And how about the entrance? He popped out of a high tower in one corner of the stadium. Then, a moment later, he emerged from atop a football goalpost. Then in another distant corner: Michael Jackson again! It was grand; it was impressive. But it also had just a hint of "Notice me. I am godlike. I am to be admired and worshiped."

Yes, the secular world has some of this in its entertainment. And we're not going to spend time howling at the moon about things that can't be changed. But do our musicians in our churches ever fall prey to this exact temptation?

I'm aware, certainly, that sometimes people clap after a special music in church. I've had TV makeup put on my face before, and I've felt the tug of faint pleasure at standing in a spotlight. I confess—I've had to fight this thing too. There's something very pleasant about being a star, about even a trace of celebrity status. I can get to liking it, seeking it, using it. Some of that just happens, and you deal with it. But I know in my own life that there's a difference between "Here's Pastor Smith; let's give him a warm welcome" and "Ladies and Gentlemen, the moment you've been waiting for . . . heeeeeere's David! And he's available for autographs!" God help me to ever avoid seeking or wanting or expecting the slightest bit of that.

Did you know that the word "glorify" or "glorified" happens in the Word of God a total of 25 times? There's one verse where God talks about bringing glory and honor to His house, His temple. And one verse, Jeremiah 30:19, where God says He will glorify His people. But in all of the other 23 references, do you know who the subject is of that verb "glorify"? It's God Himself, of course. Friend, our purpose on this earth is to glorify Him, to bring honor to Him, to bring worship and praise to Him. I have no problem at all with "praise and worship" music, if it properly and appropriately gives the praise and the worship to the place it belongs: the throne of heaven.

Probably our favorite of those 25 verses is one that gets quoted a lot at the Voice of Prophecy, probably to keep us humble after the TV makeup lady leaves the building. Matthew 5:16 is an invitation from Jesus Himself, and what good counsel for anyone who plugs in a guitar at church or adjusts the stops on the pipe organ. *"Let your light so shine before men, that they may see your good works [or music], and glorify your Father which is in heaven"* (KJV).

Isn't that beautiful? Listen, that verse encompasses our lives on a 24/7 basis, but it certainly hits the one hour on Sabbath or Sunday morning at church. If the congregation applauds after your number at church—fine, acknowledge it. But pass it right along to God. If they say amen, or compliment you, or lift you up in any way, follow the advice of that recent hit from *The Preacher's Wife*—"I'll Hasten to His Throne"—and deposit the glory there.

Bill Johnsson, in his *Adventist Review* editorial, affirms much of what our young people are doing in churches these days, but lists as Number One this guideline, which I want to quote word-for-word: "In church, singing and all music should be worship, never a performance. Anyone who seeks to draw attention to themselves by gyrations or organ theatrics is out of place."

So if you want some applause for yourself, pick up a trombone and head over to Preservation Hall. On the other hand, if you want to bring glory to God and His Son Jesus, drive with me over to church and let's surrender self and spotlights together.

Zombie Listeners

It was an electric Monday night in Abilene. The Christian rock-and-roll band, Audio Adrenaline, was performing for thousands of teenagers. And lead singer Mark Stuart got the troops whipped up with this exhortation: "I see you jumpin' and sweatin' and screamin' for Jesus Christ."

And then the music played. High in decibels; high in energy; high in beat; high in movement. Another band playing that night, the Supertones, had its lead singer, Matt Morginsky, tell the crowd: "Rock your heads off. We'll stay on stage on one condition—everyone here dances."

And they did. The reporter covering the event commented about what happened next: "But while the music rocked, the place got quiet as, dare I say, a church when band members gave words of encouragement to the mostly teen-age and college-age crowd."

And at a lot of these events—which are happening more and more now—the loud rock-and-roll music is being followed by a sermon. Auditoriums go from 140 decibels to two decibels; you can hear a pin drop as a drummer gives an appeal for people to surrender to

Christ. You can hear weeping. You can hear drugs and promiscuity being surrendered.

And yet . . . it's happening to the tune of rock music. Loud rock music. And onlookers from the Geriatric Generation—middle-aged preachers like me—have to wonder aloud: "Is this for real? With all the noise going on here in Abilene, and in our own backyards, our own churches now, is anything of substance getting through to anybody's brain?" After all, this concert by Audio Adrenaline (even that name says a lot, doesn't it?) is part of what they are calling "The Zombie Tour." And zombies, as we know, are usually thought of as unthinking, unaware beings that stumble through the darkness, their glazed-over eyes not seeing the realities around them. That's a zombie. Are the people who worship on so-called Christian rock music also zombies?

(Their song, by the way, "Some Kind of Zombie," actually expresses their desire to be dead to SIN, to follow with single-minded purpose, the promptings of God. "I'm enslaved to what You say.")

There are some verses of Scripture that have a direct bearing on the issue of music—and of zombies. Probably the most potent is found in 1 Corinthians chapter 14. Christians tend to debate about this chapter in the Bible, because the Apostle Paul is writing about the controversial practice of speaking in tongues in church. But here in verse 15 he addresses music: *"I will sing with my spirit, but I will also sing with my mind."*

Paul was a great believer in thinking Christianity. Well-reasoned faith. He didn't write the Old Testament verse, "Come, let us reason together," but I imagine he quoted from it in his sermons. He believed and taught that spiritual gifts, properly used in the church, should impact the mind. Should purify the thoughts, elevate the powers of decision.

Interestingly, Bill Johnsson went right to this very relevant Bible passage, 1 Corinthians 14:15, as a lead-in to his essay. In fact, his title is "Singing With My Mind." And then, as he takes us through some of the pros and cons of what we admittedly call the "music wars," he returns to the same point at the end. "Loud music that drowns out the words misses the mark," he writes. "I want to sing with the spirit, but also with my mind. That also means that if the choir sings in Latin, I need a translation."

That seconds, really, what Paul says in his letter to the Romans: *"Faith comes by hearing, and hearing by the word of God"* (Romans 10:17, NKJV).

Not too many months ago, right here in Thousand Oaks, one of our churches hosted a Friday evening contemporary concert for the young people. And my wife Lisa and I, who are only about thirty years over the targeted age demographic, looked in the mirror and said: "We're still cool. We're still groovy people. Let's go." So we did. But after about three songs, we left. Because, as even my 16-year-old daughter, Karli, admitted in frustration later, it was nothing but noise. You simply could not decipher words coming through the wall of sound. Just three instruments—guitar, bass, drums—but all three were cranked up to "high," and the words of the songs, which might well have had a gospel message, just did not penetrate people's minds. And I crept out to the parking lot feeling very old and even a bit discouraged.

But it's important, in exploring very earnestly this difficult, divisive subject, to not pit one generation against another. Let's not exclusively condemn the musicians with the Fender guitars and the people who attend their concerts. What about the time you and I sit in church where the music is quiet and reflective . . . but we allow our minds to wander out the window to the nearest golf course? You can be a zombie just as quickly around a pipe organ as you can at an Audio Adrenaline concert. The congregation is singing the opening hymn, but we're still reading the gossip news in the church bulletin, and don't join in until the last verse. Or we don't sing the opening hymn, because we're not even at church yet! We slept in, dawdled in the shower, got there late, and didn't really get to our pew until after the offering was collected. Did the message of the opening hymn reach our mind? Obviously not. Our mind was still out with our body somewhere on the 101 Freeway. My point is that all of us, whatever our musical tastes, need to make a commitment to God—that we'll offer Him our brains as well as our born-again hearts.

I've resolved that whenever I can worship God in song, I want to seize every opportunity. I don't want to just sit there in church, while others sing. I don't want to have my lips move, but not my brain cells. As Bill Johnsson says, "I will sing with my spirit, but I will also sing with my mind."

And one more point. We sometimes criticize today's music because it's loud; and certainly there is a thing as TOO loud if the sound waves simply overwhelm the human mind. That can happen; it's occurred in my life and probably in yours. That doesn't mean that energy in worship is wrong; in fact, I would suggest to you that energy in worship is consistently Scriptural, if you read through the book of Psalms.

Some Internet criticisms of what we call "Christian

rock" have been drifting into our offices; I've quoted from a recent book being compiled out of some email files. Back to the loudness issue, this one writer observes: "If the volume or dissonance of the music are such that the words cannot be heard clearly, then the whole performance is an exercise in futility."

True enough. He continues: "Unfortunately, the energy released by rock music engages feelings rather than reason."

And even though that's certainly not true of all praise music, this is the challenge we face as we go to church, or as we crank up the volume on the CD player in the car. Where does the energy in our music take us? What happens as that miracle mix of notes, rhythms, beat, lyrics, chords, etc., embeds itself inside of us? In Bill Johnsson's editorial, he makes this startling assertion—it's the third of his four vital points: "Energy is KEY. Energy doesn't necessarily mean loud; it means intensity and focus, giving God our best."

Isn't that what you want? It's certainly what I want. Good energy. I want the Christian music I hear to have energy, and to stir energy inside of me—energy of intensity in my worship. Energy of intensity and focus in my thinking. Energy in my enthusiasm, that my singing or participating or clapping will give worship up to God in a thinking, comprehending—but still mysterious and miraculous—kind of way. I want to sing like I mean it, and sing like I care.

I'm thankful for the kindred expression of interest in mindful worship from a young musician named Steven Curtis Chapman, whose concerts sometimes penetrate the stadium's top deck in terms of decibels. But he reveals in his new book entitled *Speechless: Living in Awe of God's Disruptive Grace*, about his deepest goal: "Just last night after performing a concert," he writes, "I met a woman who explained through her tears how God had used one of my songs to 'save her life' after the deep despair arising from the untimely death of her husband." Then he continues: "Each time I hear a story like that I am astonished. Never do I take such testimonies for granted because I know it has nothing to do with me. God has allowed me to see firsthand how tenaciously and tenderly He pursues the weary and brokenhearted, and somehow, through a combination of the right lyric and the right melody He accomplishes things of eternal worth."

Notice how Chapman acknowledges the power of the words to change a life. Now, what responsibility does this put upon him? Here's a bit more: "This is why I work so hard at songwriting, to achieve that delicate balance. The marriage of words and melodies is a gift that God has entrusted to me, and I have no greater joy than watching God use the fruit of my craft for His glory."

Those three words tell it all, don't they? "For HIS glory."

Song Services at Dodger Stadium

There was a complaint floating around a few years ago entitled "Why People Don't Want to Go to Ballgames Anymore." And the writer pointed out in disgust that the stadium was always too crowded; you couldn't get a good seat. The acoustics were bad. A lot of lookie-loos, not true fans, would show up just for special events like Free Hot Dog Night and clog up the place. Parking was difficult. You sometimes had to drive twenty, thirty miles just to get to the stadium.

Then, once you got there, games went too long; instead of stopping at the expected time, teams would often go into extra innings, or sudden-death overtimes. Who wants to stick around for that when you're tired and want to get home for dinner? And the kicker, certainly, was when he observed in frustration that the Dodgers—or whatever team this was—was only interested in his money. Money, money, money! They were constantly trying to get green stuff out of his wallet. Why should anyone go to a place where all they want is your hard-earned cash?

So . . . that's why nobody ever goes to baseball games

anymore. That clearly explains why, in 1997, there were only 62,616,312 people who drove a long way, sat in uncomfortable seats for events that went three-plus hours, with climates that were often too hot or too cold, with lousy, crowded restrooms that had long lines, and deliberately put themselves in an environment where the people up front wantonly and blatantly tried to get money out of them.

Well, I have no doubt that you noticed the thinly disguised moral to the above essay. Sixty-two-plus million people drive a long way to go to a place where the worship service, shall we say, runs three or four hours, where it's hard to see, difficult to hear, where thieves and sinners are sitting right next to you, Christmas-and-Easter hypocrites who only show up for the World Series and not the dog-days-in-August UN-crucial games, where people are always standing up, sitting down, moving around, blocking your view, and where beer vendors pass the plate—in a manner of speaking—about every ten minutes. Only 62 million people managed to survive that... and yet the very same excuses keep Americans out of church on Sabbath or Sunday morning in DROVES.

Oh, by the way, I should mention that there surely are fans at Dodger Stadium who really can't stand the music of Nancy Bea Heffley on the stadium organ. She's always doing *Master of the House* from "Les Miz," and in the eighth inning a clap-along Tijuana song from south of the border. Same old stuff all the time. And on an ORGAN! Who wants to hear that? But 62 million people, even if they don't like the music, manage to get through a major league baseball game.

Well, today, in churches all around North America, and the world as well, many "fans," if we can borrow

SONG SERVICES AT DODGER STADIUM

that word, are heading for the parking lots. They're switching to another team. They're changing to a different ballpark with a different organist at the stadium console. Or to a stadium where they allow drums. What we call the "music wars" has created a migration, a shift, not only in how people worship, but where.

The *Christianity Today* article I've used as a resource all along is entitled "Triumph of the Praise Songs: How Guitars Beat Out the Organ in the Worship Wars." We learn that more than half of all Christians in America now attend a contemporary-style worship service. Not because there are more contemporary services than traditional ones—although it's very close to 50/50 now. But with the more upbeat programs drawing larger crowds, they now hold a majority of Christians in North America. More than 100,000 U.S. churches participate in a copyright/royalty program so that they can use lyrics of contemporary Christian music on their overhead screens. But writer Michael Hamilton, professor of history at Notre Dame, puts his finger on a huge point when he observes: "The generation that reorganized family around the ideal of self-fulfillment has done the same with religion. Surveys consistently show that baby boomers—whether evangelical or liberal, Protestant or Catholic—attend church not out of loyalty, duty, obligation, or gratitude, but only if it meets their needs."

And perhaps that strikes you as a "duh" statement. Of course we wouldn't go to church if it didn't meet our needs. Our five favorite words have become: "Getting Something Out of It." We wouldn't go to a ballpark where the team consistently lost, and we won't go to a church with music we dislike . . . especially when there's a good church with our favorite brand of music just four blocks over. That's a no-brainer.

Which is a point I concede, but only TO a point. Because is it possible that we've come to a place where LIKING church, or liking the music, has become the most important thing about the 11:00 o'clock hour on Sabbath or Sunday morning? If drums and guitars—or a desired lack of drums and guitars—would cause a Christian to even step across a denominational boundary, which happens all the time now, does this mean that we would choose music we like, or church entertainment that pleases us . . . MORE than Bible truth? Would we trade doctrines for drums just because we like them?

That's perhaps a simplistic observation, but let me take you back to C. S. Lewis's illustration. Remember, he just plain and simple hated all church music. All of it! On every Sunday of the year, at every church he went to. He thought it was just bad. He did not like "Just As I Am"; he did not like it, Sam-I-Am.

So what did he do? There was no stadium where he could see a team he liked, borrowing from our earlier metaphor. Did he quit the sport? No, he continued to go to church his entire life, wincing with every off-key note. But in the context of writing about music, and his admitted loathing of it, he has this to say: "I assume from the outset that nothing should be done or sung or said at church which does not aim directly or indirectly either at glorifying God or edifying the people or both."

Worship, he is saying here, has two purposes. The first and most important is to offer up worship to God. To praise His name. To glorify Him and tell Him that we love Him. As it says in Psalm 150:1,2: *"Praise the Lord. Praise God in his sanctuary; praise him in his mighty heavens. Praise him for his acts of power; praise him for his surpassing greatness."* Now, here's a list of acceptable instruments, according to the inspired Word of God. *"Praise him with the sounding of the trumpet, praise him with the harp and lyre, praise him with tambourine and dancing, praise him with the strings and flute, praise him with the clash of cymbals, praise him with resounding cymbals. Let everything that has breath praise the Lord"* (verses 3-6).

What I think we're getting at here is this: we go to church, not so much to be pleased and entertained or to sample worship moments that we like, but to worship God. Oh, now it's true that liking worship is important. "It's pleasant," King David says, "to sing praises to God." Apparently, King David happened to like the ballpark organist at Jerusalem Stadium, or whatever synagogue he worshiped in. It's good when we do like praising, and singing, and praying, and testifying, and hearing sermons. But even if we perhaps don't like some aspect of what happens at church, let's keep in mind that LIKING is not the #1 reason why we are there. We're there to worship, to get vertical with God, to send our love UP to Him. And unless you're convicted in your heart that the music there is offensive to both you and God, it is possible to worship Him at that place, even if the word "like" doesn't enter in as much as we'd wish.

Granted, church is also meant to edify. If all the music is in Latin, or if your personal make up simply does not allow you to be blessed or instructed by the music at your church, then perhaps you do need to move across the street . . . as long as you can also find worship over there, and in an arena that doesn't sacrifice Bible truth and Christian obedience. But when we carelessly church-hop, looking for a better drummer, or a church that excommunicates drummers, it might be an indication that we are putting fun, or personal taste, ahead of worship.

I've got to share with you that I've heard it all. I really have. At my Ojai Valley Adventist Church we have a "blended" service that doesn't stray very far in any musical direction. But I've traveled around; I've been in big churches and small ones. Pipe organ cathedrals and then out to camp meeting young adult tents where they ran in some extension cords and had an awful lot of electric *thump*. Yes, there were times I thought the line got crossed. There have been times I've been offended, or turned off, or even just plain bored. There were times I turned away and figured God did too.

But more often now, I'm just looking to worship. When the music's classical, and when it's the Heralds. Or Kathy Troccoli. When I like it and when I don't. Most of the time, I can find an upward moment, an avenue to heaven's court where I can tell God, even accompanied by a bass guitar, "Father, You're so good to me. And I praise You."

Two Tents at Camp Meeting

I have a spiritual stop sign to put in front of you here in Chapter Ten. And actually, in this whole book I've kind of been driving along with you in a mini-odyssey of self-examination. It was a hard decision to choose this title: MUSIC WARS. Will we split up in heaven over music, where traditional worshipers will go over to the right, and those who want amplifiers and 64-channel sound boards and monitor speakers will be in their own soundproof auditorium on the left? All across America—in my denomination and in yours too, I'm sure—well-meaning people are splitting up. Some to the right, others to the left, and a good number are now going across the street. Or they're NOT crossing the street; in fact, they're not even getting out of bed any longer. The music is so bad that they've decided to worship at Mattress Metropolitan Church, or at the Chapel by the Sea.

But here's the closing question. The last time something happened at church that you didn't like . . . did you say anything? Did you vocalize your frustration, your criticism? Grumble a bit? Go ahead and vote, and here at my laptop I confess that my hand's up in the air too.

Question number two: the last time something good happened at church—excellent music, a thought-provoking sermon, special music that touched you, a Sunday School class that was well-taught—did you say something then? Did you write a note of thanks, or stay after church in order to share with the person how grateful you were?

How many hands in the air now? You know, I realize that when it comes to music, there is a question of right and wrong. There is music that doesn't belong in the holy sanctuary. There are trends that ought to concern any thinking Christian. But at the same time, we need to look in the mirror and realize how very much fun it is to criticize and complain. To look at storm clouds instead of silver linings.

A couple of years back at one of the Christian summer retreats that a few of us rotate around to each year, I happened to encounter a woman in the cafeteria. And she was holding forth on the topic of the music in the youth tent. Not maliciously, but just spreading the word about the problems down there: loud music, strong beat, etc., etc.

Finally I got up the guts to speak. "You know," I said, "that's the YOUTH tent. And, uh, you, uh . . . aren't exactly in that age demographic." She was about 40 years past it, to be exact. As it turns out, this particular Christian—and she was a good, devout Christian woman—actually was making her way from one camp meeting to another. And always going over to the youth tent to "check things out." Always with a little notepad in her hand to record the transgressions. Well, maybe not, but certainly with a mental notepad. Over in such-and-such conference, it was all rock, she reported. And then in the

TWO TENTS AT CAMP MEETING 61

"X" conference . . . things were really bad. The youth leaders there were a complete failure. And so on.

Well, let me say again: I can sympathize and relate. I'm sure there are some tent meetings where the music is too loud, too rocky, too driven by feelings and not by thought. There probably are youth leaders who are abdicating instead of leading. And yet, when we fall into the trap of making criticism our main purpose, and our main joy as well . . . we miss a great blessing. Here this woman was spending her entire summer over at the youth tent. Not worshiping, but taking notes. All the while, there was another tent or auditorium right on the same campus where songs to her liking were being done. People were connecting with Christ; they were approaching the throne room of heaven in that other auditorium. But she wasn't there. She wasn't worshiping, because she was too busy taking notes and holding court in the cafeteria.

I guess there are two competing verses of Scripture that we ought to paste on our mirrors here at the finish line. One is so familiar, found in the Sermon on the Mount by Jesus. Matthew 7:1: *"Judge not, that ye be not judged"* (KJV).

But then just 19 verses later in the same sermon, the same chapter, Jesus tells His followers: *"Wherefore by their fruits ye shall know them"* (KJV).

Meaning that it is appropriate, especially in the church, for evaluations to be made. No, we don't know hearts. But we *are* responsible, corporately, to look at where we are journeying together. And it is fair to discuss as friends and as family the results of what is happening in the youth tent . . . and over in the senior citizens tent too. And it's fair and right to ask: What is happening in the lives of people who sing songs this way or that way? Are lives being changed? As people sing about Jesus Christ, are they getting to know Jesus Christ? Are they beginning to follow Him more closely? Does this music—in Tent A or Tent B—seem to be making disciples? Is it creating devout Christians whose devotional lives are growing stronger?

And it's also fair to ask these questions. Where is the music being sung with more intensity, more fervor? In which tent are there more people just sitting there not moving their lips? Or allowing their minds to wander? Or singing without passion, without the "good energy" I mentioned earlier? Those are fair questions as we look for fruit.

If a young man with a ponytail is up front in the youth tent playing his bass guitar, and we are tempted to criticize or wonder about fruit, it is fair to ask: Under the former plan, or over in Tent B, did anyone make an effort to get this kid involved? Was he invited to participate? Or was his bass guitar talent the first one anyone noticed? Is it possible that playing the bass guitar is his spiritual gift? And as he plays Christian songs, and the words of Christian songs become embedded in his soul, and as he strives for excellence doing something for Christ, what happens inside? All fair questions.

In that same *Christianity Today* article, Michael Hamilton writes about fruit inspections this way: "Worship music ought to be judged not by the songs themselves but by the people who sing them. . . . The job of the local church is to communicate the good news of Jesus Christ, to draw people into a living relationship with God, and to remold disciples of Jesus into a Sermon-on the-Mount shape." Then he adds this: "Any worship music that aids a church in these tasks is almost certainly a conduit of the Holy Spirit. In light of this, maybe it is time to substitute charity for condescension."

I'm trying to find a bit of that charity in my own heart right now. Are people being shaped into Sermon-on-the-Mount disciples? Are they being drawn into a living relationship with God? If that kind of fruit is growing, then I'm not eager to cut down the tree.

Michael Hamilton adds this closing thought: "It is fruitless to search for a single musical style, or even any blend of musical styles, that can assist all Christians with true worship. The followers of Jesus are a far too diverse group of people—which is exactly as it should be. We need, rather, to welcome any worship music that helps churches produce disciples of Jesus Christ. We need to welcome the experimental creativity that is always searching out new ways of singing the gospel, and banish the fear that grips us when familiar music passes away. For this kind of change is the mark of a living church—the church of a living God, who restlessly ranges back and forth across the face of the earth seeking out any who would respond to His voice."

That's beautiful, isn't it? If we've got two tents at camp meeting here below, will we keep splitting up in heaven too? And will saints up there wander over to the contemporary service with little note pads?

I don't know how God will resolve music questions up there. But I know that Jesus is going to be there. Whatever service He is at, I want to be there, and I believe you want to be there, and that bass-guitar kid with the ponytail wants to be there. If we sing "Shine, Jesus, Shine," I want to be in the heaven where they sing it to the Jesus who is present. If we sing "Fairest Lord Jesus" with a pipe organ and an angel choir, and Jesus is there, then I want to be there too. Don't you desire to be where Jesus is, and worshiping Him wherever He can be found?

Closing metaphor. A person goes into a restaurant, let's say. He sits down, and proceeds to endlessly criticize everything. The service is bad, the silverware isn't properly cleaned, or lined up right according to Emily Post. The parsley should be on the left, not on the right—everybody knows that. The dressing should already be on the table, etc., etc., etc. And finally someone concludes: a person that devoted to criticism rather than eating ... really isn't very hungry. If you're truly hungry, hungering and thirsting for something, it doesn't matter that much where the parsley goes.

And if you're intensely interested in worshiping Jesus, in praising His wonderful name, you're not going to insist upon a subdivided heaven.